TOM MILLER

Can a Coal Scuttle Fly?

words by
Camay Calloway
Murphy

**Maryland Historical
Society**

Baltimore

My name is Tom Miller. I was born in Baltimore, in Maryland. My Mom says that I liked color from the beginning. She brought me home from the hospital in a bright red baby blanket. When I peeked out from the blanket and saw the colored brick houses and rows and rows of white marble steps, my little feet began to kick and my fists pummeled the air in joy. I smiled a baby smile at the pink and blue flowers inside the "Clean Block" tire urn on the sidewalk outside the house.

"His name is Tom," said my Mom. Oh, isn't he pretty," said the neighbors and friends as they circled and purred around me.

"Mom says 'pretty is as pretty does' and all *he* does is cry!," my brother said, with a scowl.

Pretty soon I learned to crawl, so my Mom went to Lafayette Market and found a big cardboard box for me. My brother carried the box home by putting it over his head and bumping into people.

Then my Mom
decorated the box
with birds and
flowers and stars
and shells.

It was my "play-
inside-so-you-don't-
crawl-off" box.

In the summer I watched my Mom paint
our whole backyard. She painted the tables
orange, the benches red, the brick walk pink,
and the fence bright green. The little side
chairs were painted purple and yellow.
She even painted the clothesline black to
make it disappear.

All the neighbors and relatives liked the bright colors of the yard. They laughed and danced around big bowls of pinkish, orange-colored hard-shelled crabs and bright red watermelon and creamy white potato salad.

My brother chased me around the yard with a crab claw. Finally my cousin showed me how to chase him back with a *whole* live crab.

That fixed him.

When I was a little bigger and ready
to go to kindergarten I was afraid.
But my father said, "Don't be afraid.
I'll make you a fine green-striped
suit to wear."

My father was a good tailor. He could
make a suit to fit any man just right.
He made me a suit to wear to kindergarten, but he was busy with his
customers and in a little bit of a hurry.

WELCOME

I thought my green and white
suit looked great. Then my
brother fell on the floor laughing
because one leg was shorter
than the other and the sleeves
were too long. But the kindergarten teacher said, "Tom, you
look like a little gentleman."
When I heard that I just kicked
my feet in a dance and pummeled the air with my fists.

When I was about ten years old my brother and I became huntin' buddies. We had a neighbor who saved a lot of what we called "treasures" and other folks called "junk."

She let us hunt in her garage and go home with "the good stuff." We got a metal toolbox that a car had run over, a torn lampshade, and a footstool with a foot missing. One day I found a bent coal scuttle.

A coal scuttle is a bucket with a long lip that people used in olden times to throw coal into their furnace or stove for heat. This coal scuttle was truly a thing of beauty. But it looked sad, like no one wanted it.

Most times my brother would say something like "I'll fix this big part, Tom. You just hammer the nail in the chair."

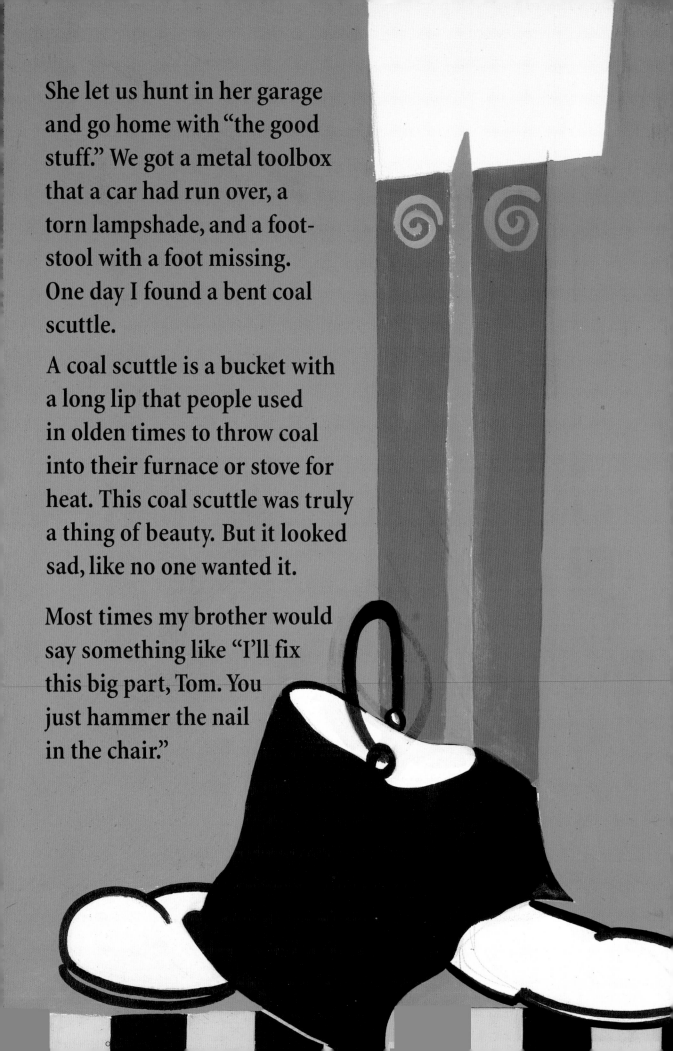

"I'll fix the coal scuttle by myself,"
I told my brother. I didn't want him
to touch that treasure.

I decided to brighten it up with
some paint. As I was painting
I thought to myself "this scuttle
looks like a bird."

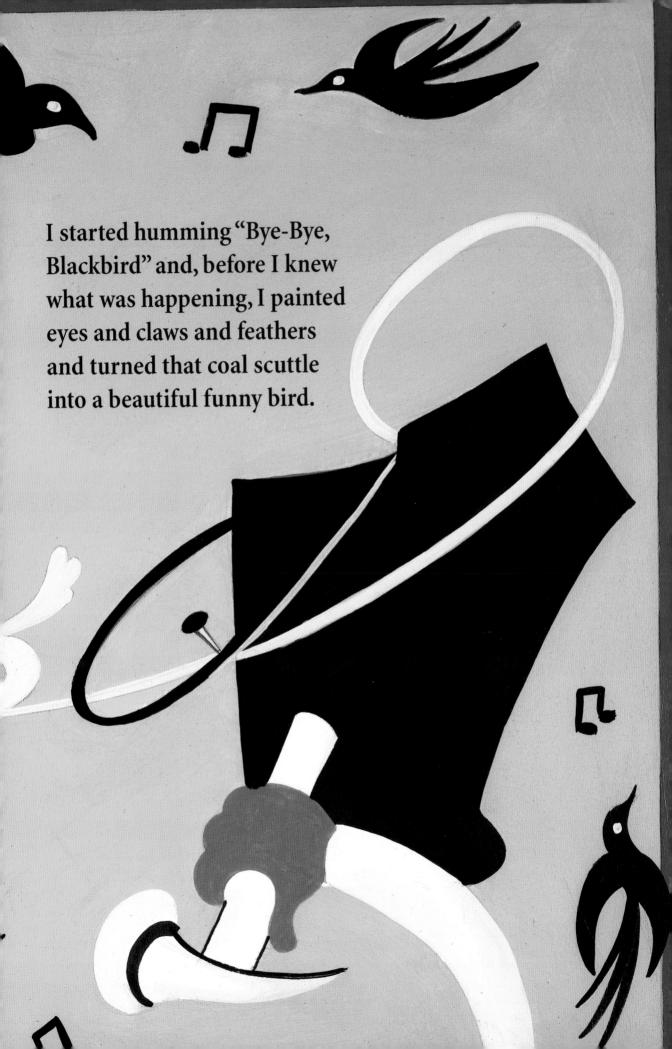

I started humming "Bye-Bye, Blackbird" and, before I knew what was happening, I painted eyes and claws and feathers and turned that coal scuttle into a beautiful funny bird.

I took it downstairs to surprise my Mom, but
my brother yelled "Oh Mom, look at this. Tom is
an artist. This is good. Real good!"

My Mom smiled.

"Hey, Tom, I'll give you fifty cents for it,"
my brother said.

"Seventy-five," I answered.

"Too high!," my brother snorted.

I didn't want to sell it anyway.
I really wanted just to look
at the coal scuttle. My Mom
put it in the living room for
everybody to see every day.

THE CARVER BEARS

When I went to high school I painted all the scenery for the plays, decorated the bulletin board, and drew pictures for my friend's book reports.

The art classes didn't have many supplies, but the teachers gave us lots of time and attention.

One day my teacher said, "Tom you must go to college at the Maryland Institute of Art. You are really good with color and design."

"Okay," I said, "but that is on the other side of town and a long way from my house."

When I first went to the Institute of Art I felt a
little bit like the coal scuttle. I felt dark and dented
and in the wrong time and place.

The other students painted with pale
soft colors, like their faces. I painted with
bold bright colors—red, blue, black,
like my neighborhood.

I was surprised when the professor said
both ways of painting are good.
"Pale soft is good, and bold bright is good.
You must paint as you see and feel.
You must tell your own story in anything
you paint," the professor said.

I thought about the coal scuttle.
I had told a story with it. I had used an
old thing that no one wanted to tell a
new story.

After a while I felt more comfortable and happy at the Institute of Art and made friends from many different cultures. My friends knew that I liked to hang pieces of canvas together to make screens and to make sculptures that were like my paintings.

Later, when I was a teacher in the Baltimore schools, I always told my students that you can make art with almost nothing. If you have no scissors, tear the paper. If you don't have the color you want in your paintbox, find the color in a magazine and paste it on your picture.

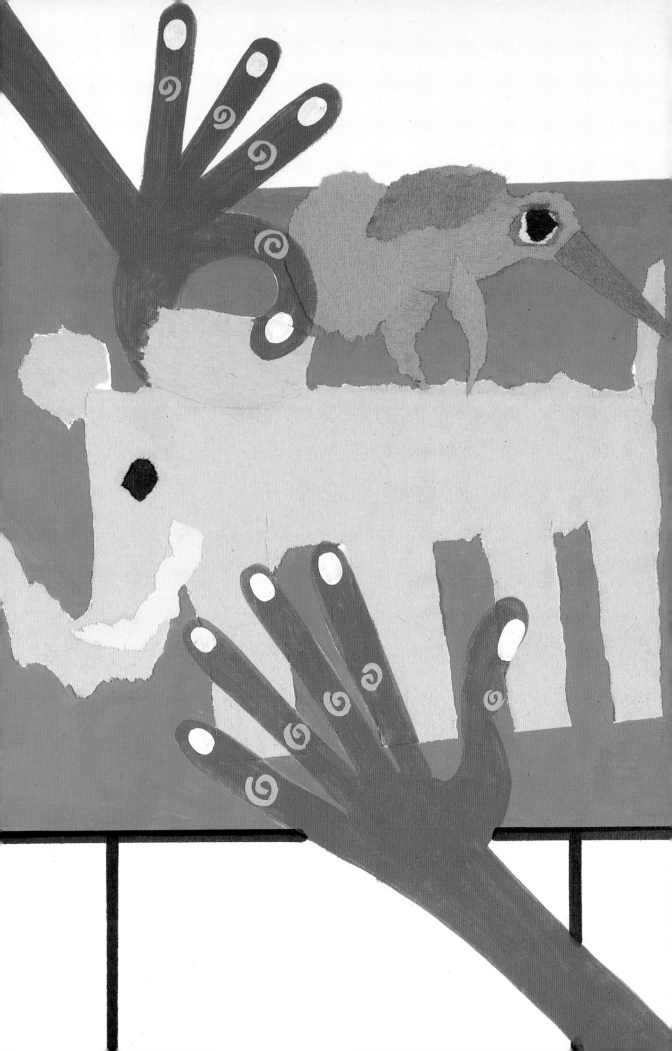

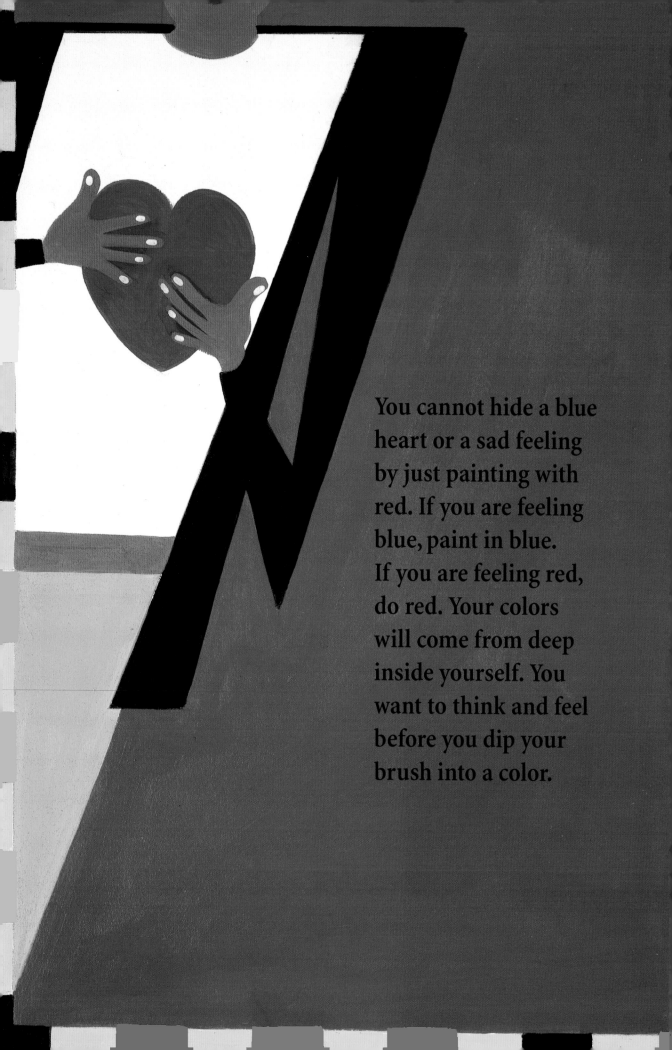

You cannot hide a blue
heart or a sad feeling
by just painting with
red. If you are feeling
blue, paint in blue.
If you are feeling red,
do red. Your colors
will come from deep
inside yourself. You
want to think and feel
before you dip your
brush into a color.

Anything is possible when you are true to your colors and true to yourself. In my studio I paint day and night. I still find many old discarded things that have beautiful shapes. I use all of these pieces to tell stories. I still like to use bright colors and make pictures and sculptures that say something about my people and my culture.

Today, some of my art is in museums and people's houses. I painted a large picture on a wall in the city of Baltimore and people now say, "Oh! That's by Tom Miller."

Many people seem to like my art. That keeps me well and working. I still like to find things like coal scuttles that I can change into art that makes others happy.

Remember, hope, love,
hard work and lots of color
can make your feet kick
with dance and your fists
pummel the air with joy.

Hope, love, hard work,
and color once made even
a poor, sad coal scuttle fly.